Mary's

An Advent Journey

Emily Owen

First published 2011

Copyright © Emily Owen 2011

All Bible verses quoted throughout
this publication are taken from the
New International Version
or the New Living Translation.

ISBN 978-0-9569796-0-5

With love to Mum

*thank you for always making
advent special*

See, your Saviour comes…

Isaiah 62 v 11

Introduction

Advent is one of my favourite times of year. I enjoy the advent candles, advent rings, advent services, nativity plays...in short, the advent I know is a wonderful time, full of expectation as I anticipate the birth of Jesus.

But what about the very first advent?
When advent led to the literal birth of Jesus?
How did people feel at the time?
How did Mary feel at the time?

Did Mary, like me, enjoy the whole lead up to Jesus' birth, the lead up to Christmas, or were there some aspects that she'd rather hadn't happened?

This book journeys through advent (covering 1st-25th December) with Mary, sharing in her trials, her excitements, her fears and her joys.

As you read it, you can learn from Mary, be challenged by her, prepare for Jesus' coming with her...

Each day's reading ends with Mary's Memo. This is a challenge to keep in mind throughout the day and to be remembered when various situations/people cross your path.

It is worth pointing out that, whilst most of the diary entries are based on biblical fact, a few times it was necessary to 'fill in the gaps' – I did this by researching what life was like at the time of Jesus' birth and by trying to put myself in Mary's place (I have been a teenaged girl!).

Please do read the accounts in the bible, in the books of Matthew and Luke, from which I got the information for Mary's diary.
Remember that anything not found written in these accounts is conjecture!

It is my prayer that reading Mary's Diary this advent will challenge and encourage you in your Christian walk and will draw you closer to Jesus.

Emily

1st December

I have decided to keep a diary about my life....
My name is Mary.
I am 14 years old.
I live in Nazareth.
I have brown hair.
I like cooking.
I DON'T like doing laundry.
My favourite colour is blue.

Imagine you have decided to keep a diary about you and your life.

What would you write on the first page?
What do you think is important about you?
What would you change about yourself?

When other people look at you and your life, what would they think are your priorities?

Now, imagine GOD has decided to keep a diary about you and your life.

What would He write on the first page?
What does He think is important about you?
What would He change about you?
When God looks at you and your life, what would He want your priorities to be?

Now compare the two sets of answers.
How are they the same?
How are they different?
How do they challenge you?

There is a saying,

> 'God loves you just the way you are, but
> He loves you too much to let you stay that way.'

Let's take that in two sections;

'God loves you just the way you are…'

God loves you!
Isn't that amazing?
The God who created the universe LOVES you.
Because you are you.
Even though you're not perfect.
Even though you get your priorities wrong.
God loves you.

Why not remind yourself of that as you go through
today?

When things go well – coffee with a friend, a hug
from a child, a great school report – say to yourself,
'God loves me.'

And when things don't go so well – you snap at the
kids, you do badly in an exam, there's a massive
queue in the supermarket – say to yourself,
'God loves me.'

'…but He loves you too much to let you stay
that way.'

Because He loves you so much,
God wants to mould you,
to change you,
to make you more like Jesus.

2 Corinthians 3 v 18;
'We…are being transformed into His likeness…'

Are you letting God transform you?

You could start by praying the prayer below, based
on Ephesians 3 v 17-18;

Lord God,

*During this Advent time, I pray that I will begin to
understand how wide and long and high and deep
Your love for me really is, and to allow it to make
me more like Jesus.*

Amen

Make it your prayer, this Advent, that you will
allow God to love you and to change you.

God loves me

2nd December

This is my second diary entry and I wanted it to be really exciting...but it's not. I imagined having something interesting to write about but I haven't. I got up at the normal time, ate meals at the normal time, did normal jobs, saw people I see every day...I'm going to stop writing now because I really don't have anything to say.

Do you ever feel like that?
That you are just going through the motions, going through the same old routine...?

Let's look at Mark 12;

An elderly lady is walking slowly along, on her way to the temple to give some money.

This is not an unusual journey for her.
She often goes to give.

No one notices her, everyone else is always too busy showing off how much money they are giving.

She doesn't show off.
Even if she wanted to there would be no point as she doesn't have a lot of money to give.
She just quietly goes up, gives her money, and leaves.

But....unbeknown to her, someone did notice her. Someone did appreciate what she gave – and that someone was Jesus.

He not only noticed her, he used her as an example to teach his disciples about giving.

'She, out of her poverty, put in everything.'

The woman was going through her routine, doing what she often did, nothing new or exciting…but Jesus noticed her.
Jesus watched her.
Jesus praised her, for doing what she normally did!

Nothing new or different.

And it's the same for you.
When you are doing the school run, holding a coffee morning, going to work or college, doing the shopping, cleaning the house –
normal, mundane things….

Jesus notices you.
Jesus watches you.

Never think that what you do is not appreciated.

The woman gave glory to God by simply living her life.
Her story has been told again and again…

Do you give glory to God by simply living your life?

By living the life He's given you?

Colossians 3 v 17;

'Whatever you do or say, do it as a representative of the Lord Jesus, giving thanks through Him to God the Father.'

Wow! You are a representative of the Lord Jesus!

Will you represent Him well today,
whatever you do,
however mundane?

You can be sure that He'll notice…

Lord God,

You know the things that will come my way today.
I don't.
Whatever happens today, Lord,
I ask You to help me to be Your representative, to show by the way I live that I belong to You.

Amen

I'm the Lord's representative

3rd December

I'm so excited! I've wanted something like this to happen for so long....and now it has! I can hardly believe it! But maybe I'd better start at the beginning...

It was my turn to go to the market today, so I set off quite early in the morning. It's great when it's my turn to go, I love getting away from the house for a bit.

Anyway, I did the shopping and headed for home. I had to walk past the synagogue on my way and, just as I passed the entrance, I tripped on a loose stone. My shopping went flying, fruit and vegetables everywhere! I was really embarrassed and hoped no one had noticed but, of course, they had. And it wasn't just anyone, it was Joseph! He's the man I've had my eye on for ages, he's so kind and good looking. And there he was, picking up my shopping and helping me up. I tell you, I wanted the ground to open up and swallow me! Talk about making an impression. I couldn't even meet his eye, just muttered a quick thank you and hurried home.

But he's so nice! The way he helped me, didn't make a fuss, just got on with it. And he's easily the best looking man there, and the kindest. Oh, I can't stop thinking about him!

When was the last time you couldn't stop thinking about someone? Or something?

Maybe you can't stop thinking about your endless 'to do' list, or what you can't eat because you're on a certain diet, or the holiday you're planning with your friends, or the new clothes you need to buy for the kids or even something more serious, like an illness or a hospital appointment.

Now let me ask you, when was the last time you couldn't stop thinking about what you'd been reading in your Bible, or what you'd heard in the sermon last Sunday?

Couldn't stop thinking about God?

If it was a while ago, if you've lost your 'joy in the Lord,' why do you think that is?

Maybe other things are getting in the way, life is becoming too busy….

If you've lost that joy, how can you get it back again?
How can you restore your relationship with God?

Psalm 23 v 2/3;
'…the Lord leads me beside quiet waters, he restores my soul.'

There are no short cuts – if you want the joy,
you need to start at the beginning.

If you want your tired soul restoring to joy, you
need to allow yourself to be led beside quiet waters.

Which will probably mean slowing down
sometimes, taking a break sometimes, saying 'no'
sometimes….so that you can say 'yes' to taking
time out with God while he restores your soul…

Restores your energy,
your excitement,
your enthusiasm for Him.

Restores your joy.

So you can say with Hannah (1 Samuel 2 v 1);

'My heart rejoices in the Lord.'

Lord God,

I have lost some of my joy.
My joy in You.
And I want it back, I need it back.
Please help me.
Help me to take time to be led by You beside quiet
waters, to have you restore my soul.
Restore my joy.

Amen

Rejoice!

4ᵗʰ December

Oh my goodness! This evening, Joseph turned up at our house! He wanted to check that I was ok! Then he had a chat with Dad and, to cut a long story short, Joseph and I are engaged to be married! This is what I've been waiting for, this is where I belong!

Where do you belong?
Not what bank do you belong to, or what gym, or what library….where do you *as a person* belong?

Or, to put it another way,
where do you feel accepted?
Where do you feel wanted?
Where do you feel valued?

I think Mary would have felt these things when she became engaged to Joseph. He wanted her, he valued her, he'd chosen her as his bride and he was going to marry her.

Colossians 3 v 12 refers to,
'God's chosen people...dearly loved.'

Think about it…. chosen, accepted, wanted, valued, by God…

Now think about the identity of, 'God's chosen people...'
Well, one of them is you!

Accepted, wanted, chosen, valued….you.

Let's look at a parable Jesus told (Matthew 13);

It's about a merchant…and this merchant is looking
for something. He is looking for pearls.
And not just any pearls, the pearls he is looking for
have to be the best.
So he looks and looks…and eventually he finds one.
He finds the pearl he's been looking for.
But it's expensive.
Very expensive.

What to do?
Maybe it's best to just forget about the pearl.
After all, he has many other treasures at home.
But no – this pearl is special.
So the merchant goes home, sells everything he
owns, comes back and buys that pearl.

Did you notice something in this story?
The pearl did not do anything!
The merchant wanted the pearl just
because it was a pearl!

God accepts, wants, chooses, values you…just
because you are you.

Maybe that make you uncomfortable?
Makes you think,
'why would God accept, want, choose, value me?'

The answer is - because He loves you.

Personalise 1 John 3 v 1;

**'How great is the love the Father has lavished on me, that I should be called a child of God!
And that is what I am!'**

Father God,

*I'm amazed that You want me,
that You love me,
that You choose me,
that You value me.
But thank You that You do!*

Amen

I'm chosen

Well, today is the first day of my life as an engaged woman! As soon as I woke up this morning, my first thought was, 'I am going to marry Joseph,' and then I just lay there, day dreaming....until I heard Mum reminding me that it was time to get up. And that today is my turn do the laundry. I don't like doing the laundry, having to go out into the courtyard with all the other women and listen to them gossiping and bickering. But maybe it will be ok today, I'm the one that's got news for once...
I carried the washing outside. Sure enough, there were a few women there already, so I hurried over to share my news....but, every time I opened my mouth, one of them jumped in instead. Someone's sister had had a baby, someone's brother had broken his leg, someone had had a bad sleep last night, someone wanted help with their housework...and on and on it went. I might as well have been invisible. No one was taking any notice of me and I felt as though I would burst with frustration...

Have you ever felt sidelined?

Ignored?

Not listened to?

Maybe by friends, family, church?

Let's look at Luke 18;

Jesus was very popular. Everyone wanted to see Him, whether they liked Him or not!

One day some people brought their children to Jesus. They wanted Jesus to lay his hands on them and bless them.
But, when Jesus' disciples saw them coming, they told them off! They told them to go away.
The disciples sidelined them.
They thought Jesus wouldn't be interested in children…but they were wrong.
Jesus called the children to Him.
He welcomed them, each and every one.

In yesterday's passage from 1 John, we focussed on the first part of the verse – now let's focus on the second;

'How great is the love the Father has lavished on me, *that I should be called a child of God! And that is what I am!'*

What does it mean to be a child?

Well, it probably means different things to different people but, for most children, it means to be dependent, reliant, to look to other people for help.

Now, remember that you are a child of God.
Do you depend on Him, rely on Him,
look to Him for help?

Or do you prefer to be an 'adult-child' of God –
His child in name but not in reality?
Not in a way that says,
'God, You have control of me.
I'm dependent on you.'

It's hard to be God's adult child, isn't it?

It's good to be God's child child, isn't it…
Or don't you know the answer to that one?

If you've never tried it, why not try it today?

Hand things over to God.

Let Him Father you.

Isaiah 40 v 11;
**'He tends His flock like a shepherd:
He gathers the lambs in His arms and carries
them close to His heart.'**

It's a great thing to be God's child, to remember
that you don't have to go through things alone.

To remember that He is always there to help.

Lord God,

Sometimes I forget how to be a child.
I'm so busy being 'in control' that I forget that I
don't have to handle everything by myself.
I forget that You want to help.
I do want to be Your child again, to rely on You, to
remember that You always welcome me.
Please help me to start today.

Amen

Mary's Memo

I'm God's child

Well, if yesterday turned out to be less exciting than expected, today was the other way round. In fact, I think today has to be one of the most surreal days of my life!

I was just looking after the animals. We had walked quite a way to find better pasture so, when we did find some, I had a sit down in the shade. The day was hot and I fell into a doze...until I heard a voice saying, 'Greetings, you who are highly favoured, the Lord is with you.' I thought I must be dreaming, but the dream didn't go away! In fact the more awake I became, the more real the 'dream' became. This may sound mad, but the voice I'd heard belonged to an angel. And the angel was about two feet away from me! I was petrified and also worried – why was an angel bothering with me? I blinked hard and pinched myself a few times, just to be sure I wasn't imagining this, and I think the angel must have taken pity on me because he spoke again, 'Do not be afraid, Mary, you have found favour with God.'

The story of Gabriel visiting Mary is very familiar. Sometimes, the fact that it is familiar can make it lose some of its impact.

So let's try and look at it through fresh eyes....

Mary is told that she is highly favoured,
that she has found favour with God.

Pause a minute...
Mary has found favour with God...

She doesn't appear to have done anything in
particular to have brought this on, yet here is an
angel saying that she has found favour with God.

How do you think that made her feel?
How would it make you feel?
To do nothing amazingly wonderful and yet to be
told that you have found favour with God, that you
are special to Him?

In fact, let's re-phrase that question –
                            how DOES it make you feel?
Because God also says to you,
                            'you are highly favoured.'

Personalise that;

'I am highly favoured'

'God highly favours me'

One dictionary definition of 'favoured' is
'to support, to root for.'

Mary would definitely need support during the
weeks and months ahead!

Just as Mary would be supported by God in all that
lay ahead, so, too, God will support you in all that
lies ahead for you, whatever that may be.

He'll support you, encourage you, strengthen you -
He's rooting for you!

Isaiah 43 v 1,2,4;
**'I have redeemed you…when you pass through
the waters I will be with you…you are precious
in my sight and I love you.'**

Lord God,

It's hard to believe that You highly favour me.
Help me to believe and accept that You do.
That You are supporting me,
encouraging me,
strengthening me.
Thank You that You are rooting for me.
Help me to remember that today.

Amen

God's rooting for me

*It's me again. Still reeling with shock, to be honest.
It's hard to believe an angel actually visited me!
Anyway, this is what happened next...
The angel told me I'm going to have a baby!
Yikes, I've only just got engaged.
There was the angel, telling me all about how great
this baby would be, and there was me getting more
and more confused...so in the end, I just asked him
straight out; 'Hang on a minute,' I said, 'I'm a
virgin, so how will all this stuff you're talking about
possibly happen?'*

Here we have a classic God perspective/human
perspective clash!

God says, 'this is what will happen,'
and we say,
'hang on a minute, what about x/y/z?'

One example of this kind of clash is found in
2 Kings 6;

Elisha's servant is panicking. His city is surrounded
by the enemy army – every direction he looks in, he
sees enemy soldiers, horses, chariots.

So, he's panicking like mad, and, to make matters
worse, Elisha is just calmly sitting there,
not saying anything.
In the end, it is too much for the servant...

He rushes over to Elisha and blurts out,

'This is a nightmare!
We're surrounded!
They're coming to get us!
What are we going to do?!'

Elisha replies, 'Don't worry.
There are more on our side than on theirs.'

Huh?!

The servant looks around and counts up the number
on their side…exactly none.
Well, two if you count him and Elisha, but they're
not really up for fighting anyway.

The servant looks at Elisha who, once again, is
sitting calmly, this time with his eyes closed.

Elisha prays. 'Lord, open his eyes.'

And the Lord answers Elisha's prayer.

The Lord, 'opens the servants' eyes'….and the
servant sees 'the hills full of horses and chariots of
fire all around Elisha.'

The servant didn't realise it, but God had it sorted
all the time!

What a great thing to remember –
God's got it sorted.

Whatever it is, whatever happens today –
God's got it sorted.
His way.

The servant had his eyes opened and he saw things
from God's perspective.

1 Samuel 16 v 7;
**'Man looks on the outward appearance but the
Lord looks at the heart.'**

As you go through today, try to see people and
situations as God sees them,
to look from His perspective.

Lord God,

Thank You that You have everything sorted,
that I don't need to panic.
Help me to put that into practice.
And Lord, give me eyes that see people and
circumstances from Your perspective.
Help me not to base my opinions on outward
appearances.

Amen

Lord, open my eyes

8th December

*Still trying to get my head round all this...the latest
is that it's not just any baby, this baby will be God's
Son. The angel even told me to call him Jesus. He
said my baby will be great and will be called the
Son of the Most High. What?! 'The Most High'
must mean God, right? And get this, Elizabeth is
pregnant! My cousin, surely she's too old to have a
baby?*
*My head was spinning, I could feel a headache
coming on...I had so many questions whizzing
round my head – What...? Why...? How..?*
*I think my confusion must have shown and the angel
took pity on me again.*
He explained, 'Nothing is impossible with God.'

Nothing is impossible with God.

Or, to put it another way –
Everything is possible with God.

Do you believe that?
Really believe it?

Believe that God can deal with your
confusion,
failure,
temper,
disappointment,
fear,
anger,
things you keep buried and hidden from the world?

Let's take a look at Moses;

Moses was adopted.
Exodus 2 v 10 - 'Moses was taken to Pharoah's daughter and he became her son.'

Born a Hebrew but raised as an Egyptian, Moses grew up feeling that he didn't quite belong.
Exodus 2 v 11 - 'Moses...saw an Egyptian beating a Hebrew, one of his own people.'

Moses had a temper.
Exodus 2 v 12 - 'Glancing this way and that and seeing no one, Moses killed the Egyptian.'

Moses had a terrible secret.
Exodus 2 v 12 -'Moses hid the Egyptian in the sand.'

When Pharoah heard of this, he tried to kill Moses.

Moses was scared of other people.
Exodus 2 v 14 - '...Moses was afraid and thought, "What I did must have become known."'

Moses ran away.
Exodus 2 v 15 - 'Moses fled from Pharoah.'

Moses was alone.
Exodus 2 v 15 - 'Moses went to live in Midian.'

When given a job by God, Moses lacked self –confidence.
Exodus 3 v 11 - "Who am I, that I should do this?"

Moses certainly had a lot to deal with!

Do any of his feelings ring true with you?

Now ask yourself, is Moses' personal CV one that would be at the top of the pile, or straight in the rejection bin?

Probably, humanly speaking it would be in the bin but heavenly speaking, it was straight to the top of the pile!

What made the difference?
Exodus 3 v 12; **'God said, 'I will be with you.'**

It's not a what, it's a who! It's God.

God would be with him.

Suddenly, Moses has the best CV for the job!

What's your personal CV like?
Good for dealing with the things we mentioned earlier?

2 Corinthians 12 v 9;
God says to you, **'My grace is sufficient for you, for my power is made perfect in weakness.'**

If you've got God with you,
you can deal with anything.

Lord God,

I do believe that You can deal with things that I keep hidden from everyone else.
Help me to let You in.
And Lord, I often feel like a failure.
Thank You that Your grace is sufficient.
Please perfect Your power in my weaknesses.

Amen

Mary's Memo

Nothing is impossible with God

9th December

'Nothing is impossible with God.'
Ok, so there I was, waiting for the next bit but the
angel just stopped talking and there was this
silence, that I knew I was supposed to fill. He was
waiting for me to speak. Well, I know that God can
do anything, I really do but I guess I've never really
been faced with this question before – do I want
Him to do what He wants with me? I do in my
head, of course I do, but now we are talking about
reality. And a very strange reality at that! Having
a baby was definitely not on my immediate agenda.
But it seems it's on God's….me, God, me, God, it
feels as though I'm having a tug of war! I shut my
eyes. The words went through my mind faster and
faster – me, God, me God and suddenly I sat up
straight. Of course I have to do it God's way. If I
don't, 'me and God' will come apart and I will drift
away. I couldn't stand that. I have to be with God,
whatever happens. I opened my eyes and said to the
angel,
'I'm God's. Let Him have his way with me.'

Have you ever had a tug of war with God?

Maybe you're in the middle of one right now….

Let's look at Cain, in Genesis 4;

One day, Cain and his brother, Abel, each brought an offering to God. Abel brought his best lambs, whilst Cain brought some of his crops. We don't know what crops but they were clearly not the best that he could bring.

Already we have the tug of war –

Cain wants to give to God, God wants Cain's best, Cain doesn't want to give his best….a step away from God.

So God is not pleased with Cain's offering in the way that He's pleased with Abel's, which makes Cain really angry…another step away from God.

God comes to Cain and reassures him that he can still be accepted, he can still get back on track…

But by now, it seems that Cain is even further from God. He doesn't respond to God's offer of reconciliation at all, but chooses to go and kill his brother instead…another step away from God.

Then, when challenged about it by God, he lies outright…another step away from God.

Then God banishes him…

Do you see the downwards spiral?
And all because Cain tried to do it his way, not
God's way…

God always knows best and wants the best for us.

Sometimes it can be easier to acknowledge that He
knows best in our heads rather than in our hearts!

Jeremiah 29 v 11;
**'I know the plans I have for you,' declares the
Lord, 'They are plans for good and not for
disaster, to give you a future and a hope.'**

Will you say with Mary,

'I'm God's. Let Him have His way with me.'

Lord God,

I do know that Your way is best.
At least, I know it in my head.
Help me to know it in my heart.

Amen

God knows best

10th December

*Came down to earth with a bump today. Was on
such a high after meeting the angel and realising
that God truly does know best...but today I
remembered that this is not just about me, this
involves Joseph, too. How am I supposed to tell
him that I'm pregnant with the Son of God? It was
hard enough for me to believe, and I at least had an
angel telling me! I keep rehearsing what to say but
nothing sounds quite right – 'Joseph, I've got some
news...' 'Joseph, do you like children?' Joseph is
such a good man, so respected in our community.
What will this do to his reputation? Oh, it's no
good. However I phrase this, it all comes down to
the same thing. I just have to tell him. 'Joseph, I'm
pregnant.'*

Going from a spiritual high, a 'mountain top'
experience, back down to earth with a bump when
the rest of the world kicks in.
Nearly all Christians will have experienced this in
one way or another!

Let's look at Elijah, in 1 Kings 18 & 19;

Elijah has just had a wonderful triumph over the
worshippers of the pagan god, Baal. On Mount
Carmel, Elijah showed them who the true God
really is.
God sent fire from heaven!
Everyone acknowledged God as the true God, and
He'd used Elijah to show them! And then all the
prophets of Baal were killed!

44

Elijah must have been buzzing,
feeling so close to God,
on a real spiritual high…

But what do we read in the next chapter?

Elijah is on the run.

Queen Jezebel is not happy that he killed the
prophets of Baal and she wants revenge.

Elijah is terrified and running for his life – you
could say, he's back down to earth with a bump.

Eventually, exhausted, he sits down and prays that
he will die.

And God's reply? 'Get up and eat.'

Clearly, God is does not consider this to be the time
for Elijah's death.
Eating would not be necessary if Elijah was about to
die!

It can be easy to lose perspective when things seem
stacked against you.

Remember, God has a plan for your life and
He can always get you back on track,
just as He did for Elijah.

Having something to eat ensured that Elijah took time out.

We read, in 1 Kings 19, that Elijah ate and drank THEN, strengthened by the food, he travelled on.

God knew what Elijah needed better than Elijah did. Elijah thought he needed to die when God knew that he just needed a break.

Sometimes, we need to take time out.

We need to give ourselves a break.

We need to let God renew us.

We need to **'be still, and know that He is God.'** (Psalm 46 v 10)

Lord God,

It's easy for me to think that I know what I need.
Sometimes I find it difficult to wait to hear You tell me what I really do need.
Maybe that's because I'm always on the go.
Help me to take a break with You before I reach breaking point!

Amen

Take time out with God

<u>11th December</u>

Ok, so I told him. I just came out and said it. 'I'm pregnant.' I don't know how I expected him to react. Maybe shout? Hit something? (Hopefully) say everything would be ok? But any of those things would have been better than what happened. The colour drained from his face. I've heard that expression before but never really seen it, not until now. He went grey and I thought he was going to collapse or something. When he did speak, it was in a calm, controlled voice – 'We'll talk about this tomorrow.' Then he was gone. And I was left standing there all alone. I am dreading tomorrow...

Have you ever dreaded tomorrow? Maybe because of an exam, a hospital appointment, an interview...?

Let's look at Hannah, in 1 Samuel 1;

Hannah was blessed in many ways.
She had a husband who loved her,
who provided for her, who was a real man of God...
and yet, Hannah dreaded tomorrow.

Why?

Because Hannah longed to have a child.

For Hannah, every 'tomorrow' brought another day of being reminded that she was childless.
And of being reminded by her husbands' other wife that SHE had lots of children.

So what did Hannah do?

She prayed.

She told God,

'This is hard.
I'm miserable.
I'm bitter.
I'm dreading tomorrow.'

In other words, 'Help me!'

'I have been praying…out of my great anguish and grief.'

Now, we know that Hannah did indeed become pregnant, but she wasn't to know that. Not at the time.

But still she prayed.

She kept the lines of communication between her and God open, even in the midst of her distress, her bitterness, her misery – she told him how she was feeling.

And that was ok!

She gave her situation to God.

And God dealt with it.

Be honest with God.

Let Him in and let Him deal with it.

Psalm 86 v 7;
'In the day of my trouble I will call to You, for You will answer me.'

Don't be afraid of tomorrow –
God is already there.

Lord God,

Right now, I am feeling.........
I give these feelings to You.
I want to be like Hannah, to keep lines of
communication between You and me open.
Please help.

Amen

Give it to God

12th December

Well, tomorrow is here and it's a good job I gave it to God. I couldn't take this on my own…Joseph came round this morning and said he wants to split up! I am devastated. Marrying him is all I want to do. He said he will try and keep it as quiet as possible, away from the gossipers. See, that's why I like him, he's so considerate – he knows that everyone would blame me and he still wants to protect me. But the bottom line is, he wants to split up. He said he's just trying to do the right thing.

Knowing the right thing is not always easy, but God will make it clear to us when we listen to Him.

Let's look at Daniel, in the book of Daniel;

Daniel constantly tried to do the right thing, the godly thing, in a culture that was increasingly ungodly.

He managed to stand firm on what food he ate, refusing to eat food that, according to God's law, was defiled.

He stood firm when required to interpret a dream for the King, giving a true interpretation regardless of the fact that the King probably wouldn't like it.

He saw his friends stand firm, even though refusing to worship an image of gold meant they would be thrown into a fiery furnace.

You could say that Daniel knew about standing firm, about doing the right thing!

And then comes another test – don't pray to anyone except the king for the next 30 days.

Here is a problem.

Daniel always prayed to God three times a day by his open window. Anyone could see him.
So, what to do?
Maybe it would be ok to shut the window when he was praying, or pray in a different room…
he wouldn't stop praying to God, just try and hide it a bit.

But no! Daniel put God first.

He didn't change his routine.

He did the right thing…and just carried on regardless.

Which got him thrown into a den of lions.

Which allowed him to see God work mightily by shutting the lions' mouths so they didn't hurt Daniel.

Which led to the king turning to the living God.

Which led to the king telling everyone in the land about the living God.

All because Daniel did the right thing
and stuck with God.

Psalm 84 v 10;
**'A single day in Your courts is better than a
thousand anywhere else.'**

If Daniel hadn't done the right thing, if he hadn't
listened to God, he'd have missed out on seeing
God work in amazing ways.

If we don't do the right thing, if we don't follow
where God leads, we will miss out on seeing just
how mighty God is.

Lord God,

*Please help me to listen to you so that I can do the
right thing and do whatever you want me to do,
even when it's hard.
I don't want to miss out!*

Amen

Do the right thing

13th December

*Well, here's a change – my last diary entry seems
like a distant nightmare. Everything is sorted now!
Joseph had a visit from an angel, too, only his was
in a dream. The angel basically told him the same
thing he'd told me, and, I have to say, Joseph isn't
one for hanging around once he's made up his
mind. As soon as he woke up, he came round to our
house and said he was taking me home with him!
Now I'm his wife! When we got home, I asked him
what had changed his mind. 'Apart from being
given a vision by God, you mean?!' (He thinks his
jokes are really funny.) Then he told me that it was
actually four little words from God – 'Do not be
afraid.'*

Let's look at Joshua, in the books of Deuteronomy
and Joshua;

Joshua was Moses' assistant.

He led the troops in battle at Moses' command…

He went up a mountain with Moses and witnessed
the awesome presence of God….

He saw Moses' righteous anger at the Israelites
when they worshipped a golden calf…

And suddenly, Moses, Joshua's mentor, leader and
friend, is dead.

Not only dead, but leaving a daunting legacy. The book of Deuteronomy concludes with these words,

'No one has ever shown the mighty power or performed the awesome deeds that Moses did in the sight of all Israel.'

Moses must have been an amazing man…

Then, turn the page to Joshua chapter 1, and God is commanding Joshua to take over!

Take over from Moses?

Be Moses' assistant, ok.
Work with Moses, ok.
Learn from Moses, ok.

But take over from Moses??

Now that's different.

And what does God say to Joshua?

'Do not be afraid.'

And when God says, 'Do not be afraid,'
He means it!

There's no need to be afraid when God's with
you...

So Joshua steps up to the plate and tells the people,

'Get ready, we're going.
I'm going God's way...I'm not afraid.'

Psalm 56 v 3/4;
**'When I am afraid, I will trust in You...I will not
be afraid.'**

Lord God,

Sometimes life is hard.
I get worried.
I get scared.
Help me to say with the psalmist,
'when I am afraid, I will trust in You'
...and please help me to do it.

Amen

Don't be afraid

14th December

My life is a roller coaster at the moment, up down, up down! Yesterday was definitely an up but today is a down. I thought people would at least try and be happy for me but, no. It's not only that they aren't happy, they're definitely NOT happy. People walk by me on the road as if they haven't seen me, though I know they have. They break into huddles round the cooking pots and don't let me in. If people do speak to me, it's just to be rude and call me crazy. I know it's 'cos I'm pregnant but, when I try to explain, they don't want to know. Joseph found me in the house crying earlier and what he said brought me such comfort. He told me that, not only did the angel tell him not to be afraid, he told him what the baby will be called. In fact, he'll have lots of names. One name will be Jesus, one name will be Immanuel...I looked at Joseph, wide eyed. 'Yes', he said, 'Immanuel, meaning, God with us.' I look down and smile. He's with me.

Have you ever been ostracised, ignored, bullied for your faith?

Let's look at David, 1 Samuel 17;

The Israelite army are fed up. Morale is low. They just haven't got anyone who can possibly fight against Goliath, the giant man their enemies, the Philistines, keep parading before them.
Every day Goliath taunts the Israelites and every day their confidence sinks a little lower.

Enter David.

He's a shepherd, not a soldier.
He's only at the battleground because he's come to see his soldier brothers.

When he finds them, they all start chatting and, in the middle of the conversation, David hears a shout.

Someone is shouting, threatening, defying the Israelites to find just one man to fight him.

David looks around.

His brothers look scared.
In fact, everyone looks scared.

Then David becomes indignant.

How dare anyone threaten and bully the Israelites like that!
Don't they know that God is for Israel?
That He's promised to never leave them or forsake them?

Just as the giant turns away, David shouts, 'I'll go!'

Everyone looks at him in stunned silence.

Eventually, the Israelite king, Saul, offers David the use of his armour, his tunic and his sword to fight Goliath.

David refuses.

In the end, all David takes with him are his sling and a few stones - the tools that God has helped him use successfully in his life as a shepherd.

Of course, when Goliath sees David coming, he has a field day!

He mocks David,
ridicules David,
taunts David…
and is killed by David.

Killed by David who, to outward appearances didn't stand a chance.

Killed by David who had God with him, so Goliath never stood a chance.

Psalm 139 v 8;
'If I go up to the heavens, You are there; if I make my bed in the depths, You are there.'

Lord God,

Thank You that You are with me, wherever I go, however people treat me, whatever they say to me. Please help me to remember that; to remember that You are my Immanuel.

Amen

God is with me

15th December

I've decided to go and visit Elizabeth. She's my cousin but, probably because she's so much older than me, we've never really had much in common...until now. Who would have thought we'd be pregnant at the same time?! I'm really pleased for Elizabeth, she's wanted a child for so long. Hopefully she'll be pleased for me, too. I'm looking forward to seeing her, I haven't seen her for ages. We just don't stay in touch as much as we should, I guess, but we are family, after all. And our babies have brought us together. Well, I guess it's my baby really. If it wasn't for the angel coming to me and telling me I am pregnant, he wouldn't have told me that Elizabeth is pregnant, and I wouldn't be going to visit her....yes, it is Jesus that's brought us together.

How do you get on with other people?
In your family?
At school or work?
Your friends?
People at church?

It can be hard to get along with other people all the time, can't it?!
Sometimes people just unintentionally drift apart.
Sometimes we disagree and fall out.

When this happens, we need to let Jesus bring us together.
Let Him heal hurts, relationships, bitterness...

Let's look at 1 Corinthians 13;

'Love is patient.'
Love is, but sometimes we're not!

What does the bible say?
1 Thessalonians 5 v 14;
'Be patient with everyone.'
2 Peter 3 v 9; **'The Lord…is patient with you.'**

'Love is kind.'
Love is, but sometimes we're not!

What does the bible say?
Ephesians 4 v 32;
'Be kind and compassionate to one another.'
James 5 v 11; **'The Lord is full of compassion.'**

'Love is not proud.'
Love isn't, but sometimes we are!

What does the bible say?
Romans 12 v 16; **'Do not be proud.'**
Psalm 147 v 6; **'The Lord sustains the humble.'**

'Love keeps no record of wrongs.'
Love doesn't, but sometimes we do!

What does the bible say?
Colossians 3 v 13;
'Forgive as the Lord forgave you.'

Jesus commands us to
'Love each other as I have loved you.'
(John 15 v 12)

How has Jesus loved you?

He put you before everything else –
He gave up heaven to come to earth for you.

How have you loved other people?
By putting them first?
By loving them with Jesus' love?

How *will* you love other people this week, this
month, this year?
With Jesus' love?

Think about how you can show Jesus' love to
others.

Try it today…

Lord God,

*Thank You that Jesus loves me so much that He
gave up everything for me.*
Lord, that is amazing.
I can't understand it but I know it's true.
*Please help me to show Jesus' love to other people,
by putting them before myself.*

Amen

Love like Jesus

I'm writing this from Elizabeth's house. I arrived safely and she was really pleased to see me, what a relief. And an amazing thing happened when I arrived. I had just seen Elizabeth and called, 'hello,' when she suddenly put her hands on her rounded stomach and bent over double. I was really scared, what if something had happened to her baby? So I hurried over, full of concern, but when I got to her I saw that she was laughing! She couldn't speak for laughing, just kept stroking her stomach, and her face was alight with joy. I was really unsure what to do so I just kind of hovered next to her. In the end, she managed to tell me what she was so happy about – apparently, as soon as I'd called hello, her baby leaped in her womb. She said he was leaping for joy! I don't think I need have worried about being welcome...

Elizabeth's baby leapt in her womb when Mary, pregnant with Jesus, approached.

In other words, the baby got excited because Jesus was coming!

That's what we celebrate during Advent –

Jesus is coming!

Let's look at Zaccheaus, Luke 19;

Zaccheaus is a tax collector. Nobody likes him. He has lots of money but no friends.

One day, Zaccheaus notices there is a buzz in the air.
People seem to be excited about something.
He looks around but sees nothing unusual, except that more people than is normal seem to be out and about…

Not far away, he sees a group of people all talking at once, their faces alight with anticipation. So he sneaks up to them, hoping they won't notice, and tries to listen. It's hard to make out what they're saying but one phrase is repeated again and again – 'Jesus is coming!'

And suddenly Zaccheaus realises that he would actually quite like to see this man, Jesus.
Just see him, mind.
Zaccheaus doesn't dare let himself think that Jesus might be interested in him, no one ever is.
But he wants to see Jesus anyway.

He climbs a tree to wait for Jesus and hopefully get a better view…and then nearly falls off his branch, because Jesus stops right by his tree!

Zaccheaus can't believe it when Jesus speaks to him;
'Zaccheaus, I'm coming to your house today.'

What?! No one ever wants to come and visit him!

Zaccheaus scrambles down from the tree –
Jesus is coming to his house!

Zaccheaus had two 'comings,' or 'advents,' that
day;

He knew Jesus was coming but he had to wait.

When he went home, Jesus was coming with him.

We, too, can be like Zaccheaus.
We can be confident that Jesus is coming with us.

Whatever lies ahead of us, whatever the future
holds, Jesus is coming. He'll be there. We may
have to wait for his timing but He will be there.

Wherever you go, whatever you do, whatever you
go through…Jesus is coming with you. You are not
alone.

Matthew 28 v 20;
**'Jesus said, 'Be sure of this: I am with you
always, to the very end of the age.'''**

Lord God,

*Thank You that the story of Zaccheaus is in the
bible.*
*Thank You for the lesson that whatever happens,
You are coming with me.*
Thank you that you never leave me.

Amen

Jesus is coming

17th December

Wow! As if the 'baby leaping' thing wasn't enough, there was more to come…Elizabeth was filled with the Holy Spirit! She suddenly started speaking in a really loud voice. People were stopping to look at her. She was talking about how special my baby is and how wonderful it was to see us, how she felt humbled that we'd come but was so pleased that we had. She kept calling me blessed. I've never thought of it like that but, you know what? I am blessed. I really am. God is using me as He wants to – I don't think it's possible to be more blessed than that!

Elizabeth was in tune with God.

The bible doesn't tell us that she even knew Mary was pregnant before Mary arrived, let alone knew how special the baby was. And yet here she is, rejoicing that the mother of her Lord has visited her.

How did Elizabeth know that Mary was pregnant?

Because she was in tune with God.

His timing.

His agenda.

Let's look at Philip, Acts 8;

One day, an angel tells Philip to go and walk along
a road.
A desert road, to be precise.
No explanation, he's just told to go.
So he goes.

As he's walking along, he sees an Ethiopian, an
important official, riding along in a chariot and
reading the book of Isaiah.

God's Spirit tells Philip,
'Go to the chariot and stay near it.'
No explanation, he's just told to go.
So he goes.

And because he listens to the Spirit, because he
goes, he's able to take the opportunity to talk to the
Ethiopian, share the good news of Jesus with him
and even baptise him.

All because he was in tune with God.

And as soon as Philip has baptised the Ethiopian,
the Spirit of the Lord takes him away again!
And he ends up somewhere else, and shares the
gospel somewhere else...

All because Philip stayed in tune with God.
All because he wanted to be as close to God's will
as he could be.
And so the good news spread...

Elizabeth was in tune with the Spirit.
Philip was in tune with the Spirit.
Mary was in tune with the Spirit.

Are you in tune with the Spirit?

Do you want to obey God more than anything?

Psalm 25 v 4;
'Show me your ways, Lord, teach me your paths.'

One definition of 'blessed,' is 'granted God's favour.'

Was Mary blessed? Yes!

The same God who granted favour and blessing to Mary, favours and blesses you.

Are you blessed? Yes!

Lord God,

I want to be like Philip.
And Elizabeth and Mary.
Thank You for their deep relationship with You.
Please help me to recognise how blessed I am.
Help me to hear Your voice leading me, and help me to obey.

Amen

Stay in tune with God

18th December

Can't stop thinking about how good God is. I want to do more than just think about it, I feel as though I will burst! If I were clever, I'd write it all down. If I were an orator, I would make an impassioned speech. But I'm neither of those things. If I were a musician, I'd compose a beautiful piece of music....hang on, I can't play an instrument but I can sing and dance!

Do you ever find yourself thinking like this, focussing on what you can't do rather than on what you can?

Let's see what we can learn from Mary's song, Luke 1;

Mary 'glorifies the Lord.'
That's the first thing she does.
She focuses on God before anything else.
Always the best thing to do, whatever your circumstances!

Mary is realistic about herself before God, calling herself a 'humble servant,' not bigging herself up.

It can be easy to think, '*I deserve* such and such' –
Now stop and consider who you are before God…

Ephesians 2; **'dead in your transgressions and sins…and God made you alive with Christ…nothing to do with anything you've done, it is purely a gift from God.'**

Think about it...now try and think about what you
think you deserve!

Put's things into perspective, doesn't it?

Mary is accepting;
'the Mighty One has done great things for me.'

In other words, if God is in this, it must be good!

Mary's situation may not have been one she'd have
chosen, at least not at first, but, as she sees God in
it, her priorities, her desires, become the same as
His.
She wants what God wants, regardless.

What about you?
Do you want what God wants, regardless?

Then Mary moves back to glorifying the Lord.

What a great example, to start and finish by
glorifying God!

First, she glorifies Him for who He is then,
having brought her will in line with His,
she glorifies Him for what He's done –
she looks back at His faithfulness over the years.

She reminds herself that He is the same God now as
He was then...
a God to count on.

In his letter to the Colossian church, Paul tells the Christians that,

'your life is hidden with Christ in God.'

Paul wanted people to look at the Colossian Christians and see God.

What a great thing to aim for!

What they couldn't do didn't matter.
What did matter was that God worked through them.

What do you want people to see when they look at you?
Do you want them to see God at work?

Lord God,

Thank you for Mary's example.
Please help me to stop focussing on what I can't do but on what I can.
What I can do because I belong to You.
What I can do to show You to others because You are at work in me.

Amen

Glorify God

19th December

It's hard to believe I've been here for 3 months, the time has just flown by! It has been lovely spending time with Elizabeth, I don't think I've ever talked so much in my life – we talked about everything but, of course, mainly about our babies! It was exciting to put my hand on Elizabeth's tummy and feel her baby kicking – soon, my baby will be kicking! I know I have to go home but I really don't want to. Whilst I've been here, I've been able to forget everything, but now I have to go back and face the taunts, the sly looks, the whispering…

Have you ever been in this situation?
Scared to go back, afraid to face up to things…

What about with God?

Have you ever thought that things were so terrible that even God wouldn't want you?

Let's look at a parable Jesus told (Luke 15);

A man has two sons.

Everything is fine, they all work together on his estate…and then, one day, his younger son announces that he's leaving.

So the younger son leaves, becoming a smaller and smaller speck on the horizon until, at last, he disappears from sight.

But his father watches for him.

The younger son, in a place far away, is having a great time, making new friends, going to parties. *He doesn't know it but, back at home, his father still watches for him.*

Then the son finds that things get a bit tricky – as his money runs out, so do his friends. He finds himself alone, wondering what to do. *He doesn't know it, but his father still watches for him.*

Eventually, the son manages to get a job. Not a good job, but better than nothing. As he goes about his job, feeling more and more disheartened, *he doesn't know it, but his father still watches for him.*

Finally, he's had enough. He resigns from his job and decides to set off for home. Maybe his father will let him have a job, anything would be better than how things are at the moment. As he begins the long walk home, *he doesn't know it, but his father still watches for him.*

He trudges on. His feet are sore, he's hot, he's thirsty, he's tired and bedraggled. *He doesn't know it, but his father still watches for him.*

At last he can see the house in the distance.
His pace quickens but his eyes are downcast.
What on earth is he going to say to his father?
After all, his father had loved and cared for him for
years and what thanks did he get? His son just
walked out without a backward glance.
Will his father ever forgive him?

He's sure his father won't want him as a son but
what if he doesn't even want him as a servant?
What if he won't even speak to him?
What if…
And suddenly the son finds himself enveloped in a
big bear hug.
It's his father!
'I love you, son. Welcome home.'

As they carry on down the road together, the son
begins to apologise, over and over again.
Eventually, his father stops him;
'Son, I know.'
'But how can you know? Why would you be glad
to see me if you know? Why would you love me if
you know? I was miles away. I forgot about you,
didn't give you a second thought.'

His father stops, puts his hands on his son's
shoulders and, looking deep into his eyes, says,

'I know because I never stopped watching for you.'

Whatever you've done, whatever you've said or thought, whatever bits of you you've tried to hide, why not return to God?
He knows about them anyway, He's always watching for you.

Return completely to Him.

Won't it be great to hear him say,
'I love you. Welcome home.'

Zephaniah 3 v 17;
'The Lord…will take great delight in you…He will rejoice over you with joyful songs.'

Lord God,

Thank You that, no matter what I've done,
You are always watching for me.
You always want me back.
Help me not to leave it too long….

Amen

Mary's Memo

God is watching for me

20th December

Well, I've been home for a few months now and, gradually, things have got better. When I first arrived back from Elizabeth's, some of the things people said to me were pretty awful, but I just kept reminding myself that God is with me and that I've done nothing wrong. I went to the market this morning and, for the first time in ages, people hardly paid me any attention as I walked along, not even a second glance or a whispered remark – it was bliss!

When I got home, Joseph was there, which is unusual for him at that time of day....I should have known things were becoming too good to be true – apparently, we all have to go to Bethlehem! At least, all the people, like Joseph and me, who are descended from David. I've only just got settled back in Nazareth, and now I have to go somewhere new? Start again? Start again with the taunts, comments, whispers.....? And, this time, I am really pregnant. I mean, the baby could come any time now. How am I supposed to travel? I don't want to go to Bethlehem!

Do you know what it feels like to have to go where you don't want to go?

Perhaps God is leading you in a new direction and you want to say, 'No, stop! I'm happy where I am!'

Let's look at another Joseph in Genesis 37 ff;

Joseph is 17.
He is good looking.
He is a shepherd.
He has 11 brothers.
He is his father's favourite.

Life is good....but his brothers don't think so.

They are jealous of Joseph. They can't understand
why he is the favourite.
And then, to cap it all, Joseph has some prophetic
dreams which basically say that all the brothers will
bow down before Joseph!
This is just too much. The the brothers decide to
sell Joseph as a slave, and he ends up in Egypt.

He probably doesn't really want to go. Why would
he? Life is pretty good as it is.

In Egypt, Joseph is brought to the attention of
Potiphar, one of Pharoah's top officials, and
becomes chief of his household.

Life is good again.....
but Potiphar's wife doesn't think so.
She wants Joseph for herself.

It becomes an obsession with her and, when Joseph
refuses to sleep with her, she traps him and has him
thrown into jail.

Joseph probably doesn't really want to go.
Why would he?
Life (apart from Potiphar's wife) is pretty good as it
is.

Whilst in prison, Joseph quickly rises through the
ranks and is given charge over the prisoners. One
day, Joseph interprets some dreams, one of which
gets a man out of prison and back serving Pharoah.
The man promises to remember Joseph and put in a
kind word for him….but he doesn't.
And Joseph is still stuck in prison.

He probably doesn't really want to stay there.
Why would he?
Life is pretty grim in jail.

But, a few years later, the man remembers Joseph.
Pharoah needs a dream solving and the ex-prisoner
knows just the man to do it!

And (to cut a long story short) Joseph solves the
dream, saves the nation from famine and is
reconciled with his family.

The nation was saved because Joseph went, again
and again, where he probably didn't really want to
go.

What might God have in store for you?

1 Corinthians 2 v 9;
 **'No eye has seen, no ear has heard and no mind
has imagined what God has prepared for those
who love Him.'**

Lord God,

*Thank you that this verse from 1 Corinthians is true.
I can't even begin to imagine the things You have in
store for me!
Help me to remember that You see the bigger
picture.
Help me to trust You when You move me on.*

Amen

Mary's Memo

Go with
God

21st December

Am currently en route to Bethlehem. As expected, this journey is not easy. Joseph is walking and I am on the donkey. Have you ever tried to keep your balance on a donkey whilst 9 months pregnant?! It is hard and I'm so tired. I just can't get comfortable – what I really need is some shade but that's impossible as the sun is beating down and there is nowhere to shelter on this road. I know this sounds really moany and complaining but I am so fed up. The journey seems to be taking forever. I just have to keep focussing on the fact we're being obedient by going to Bethlehem, we're doing what's right...

Sometimes, it's hard to be obedient, isn't it?

Let's look at Ananaias, Acts 9;

Ananaias was a man who followed God.
One day, he had a vision in which the Lord told him to go and see a man named Saul, in Damascus.

Sounds fairly straightforward so far....but Ananaias knew about Saul.

He knew that Saul had basically made it his life's mission to persecute Christians.

He knew why Saul had come to Damascus –
to arrest all the people there who followed God.

Which would include Ananaias.

As if that wasn't bad enough, there was more…the Lord told Ananaias not only to go and see Saul but to go right up close to him and put his hands over Saul's blinded eyes to restore Saul's sight.

Things were becoming more difficult for Ananaias by the minute!

But God told him to go and do the right thing regardless, and the right thing was to do something he didn't want to do.

God had given Ananaias a job to do and He knew he could be relied upon…

So, Ananaias was obedient.

Ananaias went, in fear and trepidation….and God used him to kick-start the ministry of Saul, the Apostle to the Gentiles.

Saul (who became Paul) preached to, taught, nurtured, loved, cared for and encouraged a vast proportion of the early church – and it started when Ananaias put himself, his desires, his feelings to one side and was obedient.

Can God rely on you to do the right thing, to do His thing, even when it's tough?

Psalm 18 v 30;
 'As for God, His way is perfect.'

Lord God,

Your way is perfect, I know that.
Please help me to always make the decision to
follow Your way for me,
even when I don't really want to.

Amen

Obey God's way

Finally, we've reached Bethlehem! I think I could sleep for a week! The only problem is, everyone else seems to have arrived in Bethlehem, too – the place is packed. The hotels and inns are all overflowing and quite a few have turned us away. As I said to Joseph, maybe we should just find a spot under a tree or something….I can't believe there is literally no room in any of the hotels. It's strange how, surrounded by lots of noise and bustle, but with nowhere to go and no one to turn to, unwanted by everybody, I feel more lonely than I've ever felt in my life…

Have you ever felt lonely? Unwanted?
Despite all of life going on around you?

Let's look at a woman who felt just like that, in Luke 8;

Jesus is walking along, surrounded by crowds of people. He's very popular and, of course, everyone wants to talk to Him, walk with Him, see Him…

Now, imagine that you are a woman who has been bleeding for 12 years.
You've heard that Jesus can heal people and you desperately want Him to heal you. You've heard on the grapevine which way He will be heading.

You'd do anything to see Jesus –
but you are bleeding…

…and that makes you unclean, an outcast, someone who nobody wants to speak to, let alone come into contact with.

So you have a dilemma – face rejection from people, or miss out on seeing Jesus, miss out on the possibility of being healed.

The main problem is, crowds follow Jesus wherever He goes.
You've spent 12 years avoiding people and being avoided by them and now, if you're going to take this chance, you have to go in amongst the crowd.

You set off after Jesus a number of times,
but always lose courage and turn back.
You see groups of people following Jesus, chatting as they go.
But you don't have friends.
People don't want to chat with you.
People don't even notice you.

You feel lonely and dejected as, once more, you turn for home.

Then, one day, somehow you find a bit of extra courage.

You don't turn back as you near the crowd.

Instead, you quietly weave through the throng, moving closer to Jesus.

Eventually, you find yourself right behind Him!
You open your mouth to speak….
but no words come.

The old fear is back –
Will Jesus reject you?
What about all the people? When they notice you,
it will be obvious that you are on your own,
that you have no-one to talk to,
that you are unclean.

You feel crushed and deflated and, instinctively,
your hand reaches out towards Jesus.
And touches His cloak.
And your bleeding stops.
It actually stops!
Just like that.

You turn and try to sneak, unseen, back through the
crowd…but the crowd has stopped moving.
In fact, it stopped so suddenly that all the people are
bumping into each other.

That's when you hear the voice;
'Who touched me?'

You try and shrink into the ground, hoping the
crowd will start moving again, but then you hear the
voice again, 'Someone has touched me.'

Your heart thuds painfully but you know you have
to turn around…and, when you do,
Jesus is there.

You fall at His feet.
Then you tell all the people, the people who wouldn't talk to you or listen to you before, that you have been healed. And Jesus says to you, 'Daughter…go in peace.'

At the start of this passage in Luke, she is an unnamed woman -
at the end, a beloved daughter of Jesus.
Accepted, wanted, never to be lonely again –
part of His family.

2 Corinthians 5 v 17;
'Anyone who belongs to Christ has become a new person. The old life is gone; a new life has begun!'

Lord God,

Thank You that I am never unwanted, even if I feel it, because You always want me.
Thank You for bringing me into Your family.
Thank You for making me new.

Amen

Mary's Memo

I'm a new creation

*As I said, it is so crowded here. Wherever we go
people are pushing and shoving. Everyone is
desperate to find somewhere to sleep. We can't find
anywhere! As we were looking for somewhere, I
felt a sharp pain. And another. 'Joseph,' I called,
but he didn't hear me over the general hubbub. I
tried again, this time louder; 'Joseph!' He turned
round, eyes full of concern. 'Joseph, the baby is
coming!' Concern turned to speechless panic. I
wanted to shake him – 'What are we going to do?
Joseph, it's time!'*

What 'time' is it in your life?
Time for God to work?

Let's look at Matthew 14;

Jesus has sent his disciples ahead of him in their
boat, to row to the other side of the lake. They are
experienced fishermen, rowing a boat is second
nature to them.

They are rowing along when suddenly the boat
begins to tip over a bit…then a bit more…then a bit
more…and they realise that they are in the middle
of a full-blown storm.

And they are terrified.
(It must have been some storm to scare fishermen
witless!)

Then, as if they aren't scared enough, they see a ghost walking on the water!

By now they are almost out of their minds with fear…'til the ghost speaks.
And it's not a ghost, it is Jesus.

They all heave sighs of relief…except Peter. He has no time for that, he wants proof that it really is Jesus.

So he says, 'Jesus, if it's really you, tell me to come to you on the water,' and Jesus replies, 'Come!'

So now Peter has a choice.
Stay in the relative safety of the boat without Jesus or step out of the boat onto the stormy water with Jesus.

And Peter chooses the latter, he chooses to be with Jesus, he chooses to step out of the boat.

And he walks on water.

Yet, as he walks, he stops looking at Jesus, he notices again the storm crashing round him, he begins to sink…and Jesus lifts him up.

And helps him walk again.

And Peter returns to the boat,
walking on the water
with Jesus.

I doubt that Peter ever regretted getting out of that boat to be with Jesus.

Even though he did begin to sink, even though he took his eye off Jesus, even though he didn't do it all right…he didn't regret it because Jesus was with him.

Jesus was stretching Peter's faith.
It was time for Peter to do something new.
And he walked on water.

I wonder if the only ones with regrets that day were the disciples who stayed in the boat, stayed with what they knew…
and missed out on walking on water with Jesus.

What time is it in your life?
Is God challenging you?
Telling you that it's time to move on in your relationship with Him?
Time to step out of your comfort-zone?

If so, don't live with regrets and 'what ifs'.

Keep your eyes on Jesus and you can do anything He's asking of you.

Fix your eyes on Jesus and step out of the boat.

Hebrews 12 v 2;
'Keep your eyes on Jesus, the champion who initiates and perfects your faith.'

Lord God,

Thank You that, when You encourage me to get out
of the boat, You are there beside me.
Sometimes I feel as though I am drowning –
help me to keep looking at You instead of
thrashing about on my own.

Amen

Mary's Memo

It's time!

Panic, panic, panic! Joseph is dashing from door to door, begging people to let us in. I am closing my eyes and trying to pretend this is not happening to me. We are, barely, stopping ourselves from becoming hysterical. The baby is coming! We've been turned away countless times now. Joseph is knocking on yet another door. I am surprised that we are not turned away immediately but, after some conversation, are led inside...and through the house...past the sleeping area.... What's going on? Then I see the stable, smelly and full of animals. Joseph is pointing to it and nodding. Suddenly I realise! You've got to be joking, I can't give birth there!

In the scheme of what Mary had already been through, maybe giving birth in a stable was not high on the list of difficulties. Maybe it was a 'small' thing, but she still had to do it....

Let's look at John 6;

Jesus wants some time alone, but He's not going to get it.
As soon as the crowds of people hear where He is,
they follow Him, they go where He is going,
they do whatever they can to be with Jesus.

And Jesus welcomes them.
He teaches them, heals them, cares for them...
and they hang onto his every word.
Time passes, unnoticed...

Eventually, when it begins to get dark, some of Jesus' disciples come up to have a quiet word with him;
'Jesus, perhaps we should send these people home now. It's late and they'll need some food.'

The disciples clearly think Jesus is going to agree with them, to do what they say, to fit in with their timing – but they have another think coming…

Jesus replies that, not only do the people need to stay but that the disciples are in charge of making sure they get some food.
What?!
8 months salary wouldn't buy enough food for this crowd!
They look at each other, totally stumped.

Then Andrew notices a small boy, standing nearby with a packed lunch box.
The silence is becoming awkward now and none of the others is saying anything, so Andrew doubtfully mentions the boy to Jesus,
'This boy has five loaves and two fish…but that's not enough for a crowd this size.'

But, in Jesus hands, it *is*…
it is more than enough.

And all the crowd is fed.

The disciples thought they were sorted with Jesus, they knew where they stood and what He wanted from them.
So far in the gospels, we read that He wanted them to go where He went and to do what He told them, which had worked fine…until now.

Now Jesus wanted to move them on, to challenge them, to make their faith grow…

Is it time for your faith to grow?

Maybe, in this story, the boy got much more than he gave to Jesus.
Imagine the wonder he would have felt as he offered his lunch and it fed a crowd!
The boy did a 'little' thing and Jesus turned it into something big for His glory.

However small things we do or give for Jesus may seem to us,
He turns them into something big for His glory.

Mary said 'yes' to God.

Yes in the big things but also yes in the small things.

Sometimes it can be easy to think that the little things we do don't matter.

But they do.

They matter to God.

And, with God, there are no 'little' things, anyway!
Everything we do for Him is important, vital, big!

Matthew 25 v 21;
 **'Well done, my good and faithful servant. You
have been faithful in small things...'**

Lord God,

Help me to be a faithful servant.
*Please grow my faith by helping me to be faithful in
small things....*
I want to glorify You in any way I can.

Amen

Mary's Memo

*Little is Big
with God*

Jesus is born!
Finally, I am watching my beautiful baby boy.
He's perfect!
He makes everything worth it;
The shock that I was pregnant…Joseph thinking of
leaving me…the comments and taunts from the
people in the village…the journey to
Bethlehem…the feeling of having nowhere to
go…giving birth in a stable….it was all worth it.
I've held my baby in my arms at last and nothing
else matters –
Jesus is born!

Paul said, in Philippians 3 v 8 & 10;
'Everything is worthless when compared with the infinite value of knowing Christ Jesus my Lord…I want to know Christ…'

Do you want to know Christ Jesus more?

To know Him and
know Him and
know Him
until nothing else matters
because you have Jesus?

Jesus wants you to.

He wants you to spend more time with Him,
to get to know Him,
to worship Him,
to serve Him,
to talk to Him,
to let Him help you….
to remember that, whatever happens or has
happened, you'll be ok if you stick with Him.

Jesus wants you to celebrate because

He was born for you!

Happy Christmas!

A child is born to you,
A son is given to you;

And He will be called

Wonderful Counsellor,

Mighty God,

Everlasting Father,

Prince of Peace.

Isaiah 9 v 6

Jesus - born for me!